This Albion:
Snapshots of a
Compromised Land

by
Charlie Hill

*I propose a conspiracy of orphans. We exchange winks. We reject hierarchies.
All hierarchies. We take the shit of the world for granted and we exchange stories
about how we nevertheless get by. We are impertinent. More than half the stars
in the universe are orphan-stars belonging to no constellation. And they give off
more light than all the constellation stars.*

—John Berger

First published 2023 by **Culture Matters**.
Culture Matters promotes a socialist and progressive approach to art, culture and politics. See www.culturematters.org.uk

Text copyright © Charlie Hill
Photos © Charlie Hill
Edited by Mike Quille
Layout and typesetting by Alan Morrison
ISBN 978-1-912710-74-4

Acknowledgements

Stirchley, Birmingham, England; St Cuthbert's Church, Holme Lacey, Herefordshire, England; Manchester University, Manchester, England: appeared in *3:AM*, 2021—2024

Carlisle, England: appeared in *Words for the Wild*, 2019

Loch Morar, the Highlands, Scotland: appeared in *Writers Rebel*, 2021

Digbeth, Birmingham, England: appeared in *Digbeth Stories*, FloodgatePress, 2023

Leicester, England: appeared in *Collected*, Royal Literary Fund, 2022

Contents

Introduction

By Fran Lock

I first read the manuscript for **This Albion** in the midst of my own, infinitely less reflective, travels around benighted Tory Britain, and so there were moments of accidental and uncanny overlap, as if I had suddenly phased through its pages into the very places Hill was describing. This happened to me in Digbeth, meeting my post-operative grandfather for a soggy pub lunch in the shell of the old Irish Quarter. Here, Hill's description of the district's 'craft ale bars, the odd art gallery and studio, studs of Knowledge Quarter/ Creative Content Hub/Enterprise Zone/Big City Plan investment in a rubble-strewn wasteland' seemed to anticipate and capture the familiar gut-punch of affection, sadness, and anger I always feel whenever I visit. 'It seems there is an historical/ahistorical inevitability to the dereliction of all things that Digbeth's performative hubris won't help. But then maybe that's just me.' No. It's really not.

Nailing England's moments of 'performative hubris' is a significant feature of **This Albion**: the past returned (and marketed) to us as kitschy signifiers by the very forces that displace and cannibalise it: 'like a typewriter on the wall of a restaurant that used to be a print works' or indeed an ersatz tractor, artfully "abandoned" in a national park in rural Devon. In such ways does our working-class past haunt the shiny neoliberal present; persisting by pale ghostings —estates named for the trees they replaced—or as distorted simulacra, 'put on display' as Hill writes, seemingly 'to expose the fundamental nonsense of authenticity.'

This last phrase is significant, I think, in understanding what makes Hill's writing different to a number of psychogeographical musings from the past decade: these projects are often concerned with characterising and mourning a lost local or national "soul", some "authentic" local or national self. I don't much like such essentialist endeavours; to me it smacks of arrogance to assume one's own perceptions and experiences of place represent any kind of absolute "truth". There is, let's face it, an uncomfortable colonial sensibility to cohorts of predominantly middle-class men, striding about the land and pronouncing definitively on whatever it is they find there, flaunting their "discoveries", marking their territory. I've often felt that this kind of writing reduces the place it purports to signify to a mere scrim onto which is projected the author's own insights, opinions, and theories.

The daft, the hopeful and the beautiful

There's none of that in Hill's writing. He doesn't stride, he ambles, frantically peddles, clambers, or drifts. He can be awkward or uncertain, and he frequently undercuts his own narrative authority with self-deprecating humour, as when —in Derbyshire—he is forced to acknowledge 'we were hopelessly lost and in a modicum of danger; a situation that was assuredly metaphorical in some way'. Here, Hill disavows his own expertise, while unobtrusively critiquing the easy metaphorising tendency that transforms land into landscape, an aesthetic frame significant only in terms of the sensations or ideas it produces in the human 'I' that is looking at or moving through it. Hill doesn't project. He observes, aware of his own entangled subject position and ever-alert to the others around him whose experience of place may be very different to his own. Because he is less concerned with imposing a view or developing a thesis, a moving intimacy can develop between author and place, one that is perceptive, witty, and warm. One that is also *extremely* funny.

Place is not a depopulated backdrop for Hill, but a site for confrontation, constant negotiation, and misunderstanding. This allows the politics of the book to emerge in ways that feel natural and impassioned, as opposed to bloodless or merely dogmatic. It also provides occasions for humour. There is an interaction with a hi-vised bully in Digbeth (I won't spoil it) that had me crying with laughter, but which served to illustrate the extent to which capitalism's inhuman developmental agenda has ruptured not only the city-scape, but our relationships with one another.

Space is always ideological and contested. Power is control of space. On his journeys around Britain, Hill encounters every conceivable kind of impedi-ment, diversion and obstacle; sobering reminders of curtailed freedom and long, historical dispossession. In Pittenweem in Fife, an imagined idyll of escape is equally compromised by the forces of gentrification: 'So taken was I by the sight that greeted us, it took a while to register that the place was full of second-homers, I mean I'd rarely seen so many nautically-striped shirts and tasselled deck shoes and four-by-fours in such a confined space.' There is no easy distinction, Hill tells us, between the urban and the rural; our scenes of entrapment, and our scenes of escape. Capitalism's reach is total, and the despair it generates in the Howe of Fife may be less visibly writ than in Birmingham's urban decay, but it is no less present, painful or real.

Yet there is much to celebrate. Much joy in the midst of indifference, belliger-ent cruelty, and utter absurdity. While Hill is a persuasive critic of social structures, the way they infringe upon and scar our lives and lands, he is also alive to the daft, the idiosyncratic, the hopeful, and the beautiful. It is 'worth remembering that the canal was cut into the earth like an industrial wound, by working people who died in its cutting.' Writes Hill. Amen. Hill—and we —remember them best by living with curiosity, empathy, and humour.

Birmingham to Worcester canal, Birmingham, England

The canals of Birmingham—with their kingfishers and railway lines, their willow herb and jays and graffiti—exist outside the less obviously mutable suburbs they pass through: underneath too; the banks of the towpath are steep and dark and when you re-enter the city, you emerge blinking with surprise at where you are, and how different the light seems.

There's a directness to walking the canals. Although they turn corners and curve, they feel like 18th century ley lines connecting factory yards, parks, churches, and other areas of communal ritual. The Birmingham to Worcester canal is like this. From the city centre it goes out past the commercial junctions of Five Ways, through the student accommodation and apple trees of the Vale, past the university itself to Bournville, where the station is done out in Cadbury purple and the air smells of chocolate. You might see egrets here.

Just beyond Kings Norton is Wast Hills tunnel. It's a mile and a half long. Kings Norton is a parish that used to be in Worcestershire, outside the city's boundaries. There is no towpath through the tunnel and walkers are sent up and onto the Hawkesley estate, in the overground outskirts of the suburbs. Once I tried to find the other end of the tunnel, setting off past a canal side cottage and a large secondary school in the direction a heron might fly.

I didn't find it. Roads sweep through Hawkesley but it's warren-like in places too, with shortcuts as criss-crossed as the towpaths seem straight. There are discarded shopping trollies in this closely-knit patchwork of social housing, twisting alleyways and shin-high picket fences, there are desire paths, and deep scarlet haws in confusions of undergrowth. It's easy to project, to romanticise this anti-burb, this liminal space, this neither-one-thing-nor-the-other-ness, and that of the waterway that has created an underworld beneath the estate; the entrances to the tunnel are called portals, and I found Yarrow Drive led to Harebell Gardens, which led to Bargehorse Walk. But it's worth remembering that the canal was cut into the earth like an industrial wound, by working people who died in its cutting.

Albert Dock, Liverpool, England

We went to Liverpool for the nippers, and stayed in a Premier Inn on the Albert Dock. To get to it from the car park, we wheeled our suitcases past teams from France and Canada practising outside the M&S Bank Arena for the World Artistic Twirl championships. The Premier Inn was in a Unesco Grade 1 listed tobacco warehouse, in redbrick, with low arches and black steel doors and labyrinthine corridors. Our room had views over a handful of chuggy tourist boats to the Liver Building, and at night the row of red columns in front of the Tate were lit up in dazzling strips of fairy lights; it was exhilarating, in a way I imagine the best theme park in the world might be, not that I'm a fan of theme parks.

We went round a museum called The Beatles Story. It took two and a half hours and did, if nothing else, what it set out to do: by the time we left, and despite my instinctive mistrust of consensus, and John Lennon's domestic violence, and my love of free jazz, and George Harrison saying to a flight attendant 'Fuck off! Can't you see I'm meditating?', and my cultural snobbery, and Ringo Starr's support for a *Daily Mail* Brexit, and my wife overhearing a twentysomething say to his friend 'so do you think everyone in Liverpool thinks the Beatles are brilliant?', I now thought that by any meaningful measure of a quantifiably overused word, they had been a great band.

Nine Ladies Stone Circle, Derbyshire, England

I'd been to the Nine Ladies stone circle once before, and now I wanted to atone somehow, to make a sort of peace with what had happened then. I'd been young and foolish you see, and arriving to find a wafting of hippies in the prime wild camping spot, had broken out a Special Brew and a football before using one of the stones as a goalpost. Since then I've become more respectful of the past, or at least more aware of the continued relevance of its complexities, the futility of attempts to disregard it.

This time, we arrived at the stones in late afternoon. The walk along the sandy paths that cut through the heather of Stanton Moor had been longer than I'd remembered, with the views over the gritstone communities of Darley Dale and Northwood and Farley—part rural idyll, part industrial townscape, yet free of the sentimental aspect that that comes with either—more impressive; less surprisingly the stones were half the size of those in my imagination.

The location of the circle was a revelation too. In common with many sites of Bronze Age ritual, no-one knows the precise nature of its significance, but today it was easy to guess: although the stones are now surrounded by trees, the light on this part of the moor—reflected and deepened by the trunks of a bank of silver birch—was of such a profoundly luminous intensity that it could only be described as other-worldly. In another synchronous nod to my self-reproach, we arrived as a small group of people were using the circle for a wedding ceremony of some pagan provenance or other. Some of us grinned nervously at this, but I welcomed the opportunity to stand back in the trees and observe from a respectful distance.

Not that my attempt at a reconciliation with the past was as simple as that, of course. Unwilling to disturb the celebrations with our presence, we set off for a walk through the woods. The moor is quarry-scarred here, after centuries of mining for sandstone, and many routes come to an abrupt end, with signs warning against going any further. The path we took was distinct and then, as a consequence of some dubious navigation, less so. After a couple of hours, with the darkness emerging from the trees, we were forced to climb barbed wire fences and pick our way through dense, trail-free undergrowth, before acknowledging we were hopelessly lost and in a modicum of danger; a situation that was assuredly metaphorical in some way.

Stirchley, Birmingham, England

I'm getting older and have lived in Birmingham for most of my life. It's been a while since I published my first novel and I have just started writing poetry. My poems are unrefined. Shortly after I snuck one into a magazine called *Under the Radar*, I decided I wanted to place them in some sort of context, so I went to a spoken word night. On my way through town from work, running for the bus, I turned a corner and pitched into a mob just up from Holland and Barrett and the Maccy D's in Dale End; there were three stabbings that hour.

The spoken word night was in a café cum gallery in Stirchley, on the Pershore Road. It was a safe space, and sold herbed olives and hummus. The poets were young and evangelical, brimful of positive energy. The poetry was about existential distress, with an emphasis on mental health, and the audience was encouraged to whoop and cheer each poem. I felt uncomfortable. I used to know the Pershore Road—I'd wasted my teenaged years in the British Oak, the Breedon Bar and the Three Horseshoes when I worked at the Co-op and Stirchley was full of plumbers merchants selling dusty valves and shock arrestors—but I've never been much of a whooper. The atmosphere left me questioning my inability to engage with other people in this way and, by extension, questioning the value of my poetry. Was I a good fit for this scene, or surplus to requirements, a spare prick at a wedding? I settled on the latter and it helped me to relax. After all, 'To every age its art. To every art its freedom' and all that. Why should the young have any need for those who are getting older? All the old have done is drag them slowly to here.

*

In my evangelical-ish twenties I lived in Moseley above a vegan activist centre called the Aardvark. It was always before, during, or after 1994. There were many squats and heads and everybody partied; we believed that parties with sound systems and freely available chemical stimulants constituted what the sociologist Hakim Bey called 'Temporary Autonomous Zones' and contributed to a realignment of the power structures by which society was organised. We also protested against road building and the Criminal Justice Bill. In 1994 I travelled the free festival circuit with a café attached to Sybil Twirl's Temple of Unlikelihoods, a troupe of acrobats and wicker artists; when winter came we decided to hunker down and find a premises. We eventually found a gallery cum café just off St Paul's Square in the Jewellery Quarter, which was then a warren of redbrick workshops and metal bashers.

The art gallery was owned by the Revolutionary Communist Party. The Rev Coms wore cords and Barbour jackets and believed that NATO shouldn't intervene in the Balkans. We called our restaurant Vegatropolis (the 'g' is hard) after the London techno-pagan club Megatripolis. We were wary of our landlords and they of us. We were a sketchy anarchistic bunch and it took a long time to persuade them that a piece of pro-abortion art comprising a dozen red leather foetuses would be better displayed away from the main dining area. We did however, share a justifiable mistrust of the state; after we had co-hosted the first public showing of the Maltese Double Cross, a film that exposed UK/US incompetence in the handling of the Lockerbie bombing, the gallery was broken into and the Rev Coms had every one of their floppy discs wiped of data.

*

In Birmingham, the past is destroyed by steel spikes and lump hammers and bulldozed away. If it lives it is as fiction or hauntological spectres or anniversaries – matchsticks in shit—and serves no apparent purpose; even though we argue over where the matchsticks should go, the volume of shit in which to stick them shows no sign of growing smaller.

The Jewellery Quarter still has workshops but there are now as many 'neighbourhood bars' and hubs. Vegatropolis is Lasans, which has a Michelin Star and appeared on *The F Word*. Nothing came of our squats and parties and our energy—if not our anger—slowly dissipated. Maybe something will come of the spoken word night in Stirchley. I certainly hope so.

London, England

Early evening, August. I am drinking in the Craft Beer Company in Covent Garden, on the corner of Shaftesbury Avenue, at the edge of Chinatown, and the city is catching the light. *Mrs Doubtfire* is on at the Shaftesbury Theatre, *Harry Potter and the Cursed Child* at the Palace Theatre, Mickey Flanagan at the Lyric. The bar is long and the gaffer robustly bearded; a new barmaid is being introduced to American tourists with backpacks and daughters, who busily ask for directions; the beer types request samples and drink halves.

I have come down, extravagantly, for the 50-something birthday of a friend and denizen of Soho boozers. The members of our party include an ex-House of Commons tour guide who is loudly feminist, a Latvian who has put a cheesecake—or *biezpienmaise*—on the bar, and a lithe shrill boy who complains about his body and the imminence of the end of his twenties. We are joined by a tiny fella with an unnaturally deep tan who introduces himself as someone who works in the sex industry—'peep shows, prostitution, you name it'—and claims to have been arrested more times—*thousands!*—than any of his peers; when we leave to go to another pub he stops at the corner of every building we pass and shiftily scans the crowd.

In the bar, we are raucous and giggly and use the C word with relish and impunity, as though the city makes us young, and it does. We talk about the young themselves, and sex, and then, perhaps inevitably, the politics of identity; I'd share with you what we said but it's not really any of your business and some of you would use it against me.

Exeter, Devon, England

We go to Exeter to visit friends, one of whom is an artist. We have tea at their place in Topsham and he tells us he wants to leave the city as 'there's no culture here.' I am surprised when he says this but there are many definitions of culture and I don't really know the place, so I demur.

We are staying in Southernhay, just five minutes from the city's Roman walls. The area is formerly the site of the markets and is now a pleasing mix of architectural function and wit; on our way back to our hotel we pass a redbrick early Georgian terrace of town houses, some of which have been repurposed as offices, and a church from the same era that was partially rebuilt after being bombed in the war.

There's also a building from which we can hear some Sidney Bechet-esque jazz. I stop to listen and then venture into an entrance corridor lit-up in atmospheric red light. I see two signs. The first tells me that the building used to be part of the Royal Devon and Exeter Hospital, and was built in 1743, the second that it is now a restaurant called the Cosy Club. There's a menu too, advertising up-market bistro food. We are on holiday and the idea of eating up-market bistro food in a restaurant that was built as a hospital and now plays Sidney Bechet-esque jazz appeals, so I say: 'Have you seen this? It looks great! Shall we eat here tomorrow?' 'I thought you didn't like chains?' she says, and I say 'it's not a chain is it?' and she says 'yeah, there's one in Birmingham.'

She's right, of course. There are branches of the Cosy Club in Canterbury and Norwich and Taunton and York. There are none however in London, the implications of which are moot. When, exactly, does a restaurant become a chain, as opposed to a number of independent concerns? Is it when it has two branches? Three or four? Half a dozen? Do all independent restaurants want to become a chain? (I mean that would seem to be the sign of a successfully run business.) What is the point at which an independent restaurant loses the characteristics that distinguish it from a chain, and hence shifts from a position of resistance to the aesthetic and economic homogenisation of the High Street, to one of complicity in it?

The next day we are driven out to Dartmoor where our friend likes to paint. We park in a picturesque village—bear with me—called Belstone and walk along a single-track road. To our left is a cleave, or wooded valley, that separates

Belstone from Sticklepath, and on Belstone Common we pass medieval stocks that were renovated to mark the coronation of Elizabeth 2nd. Further along, in a hamlet called Birchy Lake, the road peters out into a gated footpath that leads to Holloway's Fields at the foot of the moor. Here, dotted about by the side of the road, is a small collection of old farm machinery.

Some of this looks like it belongs here. It seems to emerge organically from the manicured verges and might have been discarded by the farmers who've raised sheep on this land for centuries. But there's a tractor too, and the tractor looks ersatz somehow, out-of-place, like it's been fetched in from elsewhere and put on display to expose the fundamental nonsense of authenticity, like a typewriter on the wall of a restaurant that used to be a print works, or a bicycle on the wall of a restaurant that used to be a bicycle factory, or, if you'd rather, like a tractor in a chain of National Parks.

St Cuthbert's Church, Holme Lacey, Herefordshire

We were eating pierogi and sluicing cherry Soplica at a friend's house when we decided to go Champing. Champing is a scheme run by the Churches Conservation Trust that involves staying overnight in disused and deconsecrated churches and we were attracted both by the creative thinking that informed the initiative—'by supporting Champing, you're also helping to preserve these ancient spaces for the future'—and the potential for an experience that would surely, in some way, prove enlightening.

The church we chose was St Cuthberts, which sits in 'a pretty setting on a bend in the River Wye, looking across to the Herefordshire hills'. We wanted somewhere close enough to Birmingham to make the trip a jaunt not an expedition, but remote enough for the isolation to enhance the venture. It was reassuringly difficult to find. The last mile or so of the journey foxed the satnav and took us up a single-track road to a modern country pile where farmer's children played on quad bikes. There we parked-up and entered a graveyard enclosed by trees and hedges.

Passing under the entwined branches of two sentinels of yew, we finally saw the church itself. We picked-up the key from a small portaloo, let ourselves in and had a look around our accommodation. It was an imposing interior, a composite of the old—most of the structure was built in the 17th century—

and very old—the tower dated back to the 1400's. Despite this, it was psychically lighter than we'd imagined it might have been, with a disarming tension between the abstract and eternal, the pragmatic and the here-and-now, between the brow-furrowing substance of a 'serious house on serious earth' and the vital quirks of life.

This was underscored by our confusion over the church's status. In the churchyard, amongst those that were centuries old, we'd seen the gravestone of someone who'd died as recently as 2017, and it was impossible to tell when the place had stopped being used as a regular place of worship and remembrance. There were stained glass windows which looked ancient, another with a distinctly contemporary aesthetic. At one end of the nave was an organ with a songbook open at an arrangement of psalm 23 that might have just been played, at the other a shrine to Prince Philip—consisting of a page from a tabloid tribute, a quote from Elizabeth and two vases of plastic flowers—stood next to marble effigies from the 17th century, sarcophagi in alabaster. Camping chairs and bean bags had been arranged in the aisles, and by the collection box was a pristine laminated A4 sheet of poetry that began:

'An enigma,
Diamond encrusted beings,
Fleeing forward to an unknown shore,
I was sure, that we would be, free.

The surrounding trees whisper,
Subtly glistening in the morning sun,
They know of more than they say.'

A rule of Champing is no hot food, so we went to a pub a couple of miles up the road for something to eat. By the time we got back to St Cuthberts, and arranged our camping chairs in the graveyard, a bucolic dusk had settled over the scene. The shadows of the gravestones and the yew were lengthening while insects flitted in-and-out of patches of cornfield yellow sunlight. Crosses grew from mossy earth, birds chirruped. We opened beer and began to chat.

At first, our conversation took an unsurprising route. We were sitting in a graveyard on a long summer's evening, about to spend a night in a church. We were at the age where death and the rituals that engulf it were as central to our navigation of the world as what to have for tea; perhaps more pertinently our recent engagement with them had been both emotionally heightened and compromised by the pandemic. So we chatted about the deaths of loved ones and the funerals we'd been to, we chatted about the process of dying, the intractability of grief. Indeed, it seemed for a while that this was the dialogue to which all champing must lead. Then we heard it.

From somewhere in the trees that separated us from a field of wheat, a cuckoo called. The call was clear and thrilling. It persisted for so long that it passed from feature to accent. And whether it was because of the presence of our Polish friend, or the idiosyncrasies of the interior of the church, or this most evocative of leitmotifs, the conversation moved inexorably from the universal to the particular. Now we were considering 21st century questions, questions about England and what it meant to be English, even as the meaning of those terms flitted like fireflies in a twilight, between the living and the dead: what was unique about the idyll in which we sat? What were the forces that shaped it, and who should pay for its maintenance? What sort of people camp in a place like St Cuthberts? Or build a shrine to Prince Philip? Which of the worlds was more secure in its Englishness, and how might the two be reconciled?

We woke the next morning in camp beds under the lectern's brass eagle. After breakfast, we decided to go for a Sunday morning stroll along the river that loops around the church. As we left the graveyard, a man in khaki shorts came through the gate, cradling the camera that hung from his neck. 'She's beautiful,' he said to himself, and then 'how old is she?' Walking down the single track road, we came to a stile. A sign said 'Public Footpath', another, handwritten, 'PRIVATE LAND! KEEP OFF!' We picked our way across a field, then turned to follow a path that ran alongside the wreathing Wye, and headed back towards the church.

The path was narrow and took us between rows of crops and a dense thicket of bramble and nettle, cow parsley and hogweed that separated us from the river. Every so often there would be a gap in the greenery and we'd catch a glimpse of the water, but we wanted an unhindered view. Eventually there was an extended stretch where the vegetation thinned-out and we could get to the river's edge. We set off down a slope of bare earth, towards a shoreline of flat stones and then stopped. The water was flowing at a crawl, and cloudy with shit. There were no insects or birds, nor other signs of life.

Coventry, West Midlands, England

Out past Coventry Cathedral, towards the concrete pillars of the ring road and the new builds of the University's Business School, library and Frank Whittle Building, there's a bookshop next to a pub. The pub is called The Oak, and a sign announces there's been a building on this site since the 13th Century, a tavern since 1400. The Oak is an old skool boozer. It's many-roomed and a little bit spit-and-sawdust, a fluxus-jumble of aesthetic and function that demonstrates a grasp of the pub's unique place at the confluence of ritual and abandon.

Over its various wooden-floored levels there's a space with a pool table and a screen, sofa-like leather seating, alcoves and nooks, some of which are done out in Hallowe'en decorations. There's a door in the floor that's propped open, presumably so customers can see the crumbling stone stairway that leads to the medieval cellar. A pillar boasts a quote from the Beatles' End—*And in the end/ The love you take/ Is equal to the love you make*—and there are records pinned to the beams of the ceiling, and posters advertising karaoke and a quiz. The toilet boasts a long communal urinal, made of steel, with a few cakes of soap.

The gaffer, whose unfluent English and accent tells me might be from Turkey, or Armenia, or somewhere else in mid-Eastern Europe, asks me if I want the sound turned up on the screen. It is showing Liverpool v Everton. I don't, but he sits down and we watch a bit of the game and exchange footie chat—he supports Arsenal but loves Mo Salah—and we exclaim in all the right places.

The bookshop next door is called Gosford Books. In the window is a lovingly put-together display of second-hand paperbacks that includes Roy Porter's *Madness, a Brief History, The New Society: Art and Politics in the Weimar Period*, and *Hellish Nell: The Last of Britain's Witches*.

There are signs blu-tacked to the glass of the door:

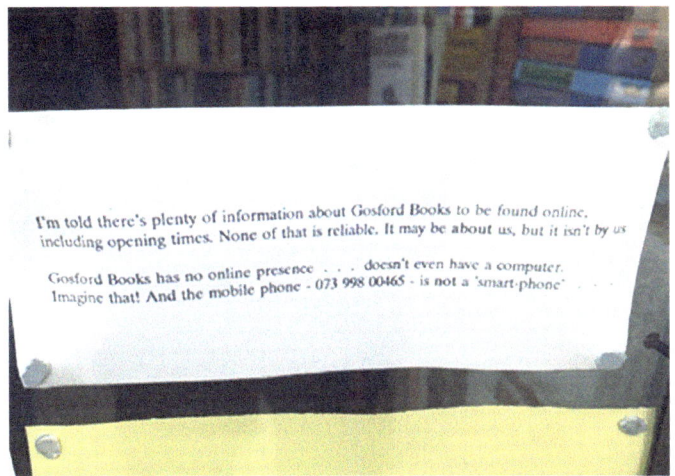

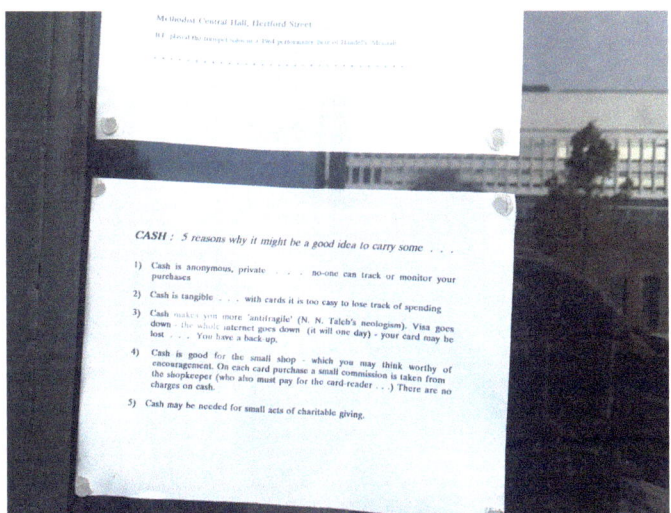

I could happily spend the rest of the afternoon here, slipping from one site of alchemical transgression to another and back again; but then the bookshop is shut and I was the only person in the pub.

Carlisle, Cumbria, England

We are in the Lake District, for a trip to Cockermouth, where we come, several times a year, for fell-walking and kayaking on Bassenthwaite Lake. Wordsworth was born in Cockermouth and his birthplace is a museum: there are many café/delis selling speciality sausages, half a dozen pubs doing real ale, two bike shops. This time, we go straight to the hospital. The hospital is in Carlisle, near an estate of red brick houses, which is being built next to the M6. While my wife goes in, I take the kids for a walk. We go along a footpath that skirts the estate, through a marshy litter-covered field, to a footbridge across the motorway. We are heading for a small wood which we can see on the other side (one of the wards of the hospital is called Coppice).

The children ask why they can't go in to see him. I tell them that he isn't well enough, but they know that this isn't the whole story. We cross the M6 by two silos that smell of chemicals. On the other side, the footpath runs next to the motorway under wires hanging down from pylons; although we can see the coppice across an area of overgrown wasteland, there are thickets of brambles like barbed wire and we can't get to it. After five minutes of walking alongside the motorway, trying to make shouted conversations fun, there is a turning. Through the branches of trees, I can just see caravans, the small ones, pulled by cars; washing is hanging on a line but it's not a holiday site, people live here, next to the motorway and we decide to go back to the hospital where we wait by the car and kill time by playing charades.

My wife returns to the car and chooses her words carefully. It's difficult to pinpoint where it started but there has been a change in him and it will be some time before he is better. On the drive to Cockermouth we go through hamlets, past empty farm buildings. Three Union Jacks mark a layby where a burger van is doing good trade with lorry drivers. We pass signs to Redmain, Blindcrake, Isel, Tallentire and Bridekirk, we pass the Moota. The Moota is a collection of prefab huts that housed Italian prisoners of war. For many years it was hired out—some time ago we went there for a ceilidh—but it is now disused and overgrown. We are quiet in the car. It has been a long drive and there is a lot to process; in the distance we can see the fells, serene.

Necropolis, Glasgow, Scotland

Usually, when I visit Glasgow, I head West: I've memories of respectably middle class Kelvinbridge, of seeing a band called the Beltanes in Herbert House, a four storey listed building in Hillhead that used to be an 'Artistic Stationery Works', of pubs with saxophonists, and a café with sofas called Manyana; this time we headed East, down to the Clyde, through Glasgow Green and past the Barras market, to Necropolis and the dead.

Necropolis is a Victorian 'garden cemetery'. It was built on a prominent hill in 1832 and modelled on Pere Lachaise cemetery in Paris. According to the Chamberlain of Glasgow's Merchant House, it was intended to be 'respectful to the dead, safe and sanitary to the living, dedicated to the Genius of Memory and to extend religious and moral feeling.' 50,000 people are buried there, with tombs and statues and mausoleums commemorating people of many faiths and races. But for all of this democratic equanimity, Necropolis also acknowledges that the gods have their price: of those 50,000 people, only 3,500 are thus memorialised, with 21,000 of the poor in unmarked graves.

This hierarchy of the dead is a continuation of the hierarchy of the living. From time-to-time there is a moral panic about the anti-social behaviour of a permanent underclass that uses Necropolis for shelter or recreation: a recent report from Leeds University remarked on the 'congregations of the homeless' on the site, and the installation of metal gates and fences to stop rough sleepers from using the mausoleums is ongoing.

From the top of Necropolis, the landscape of the East side of Glasgow is dominated by two structures with their own unique relationship to mortality and class. One is the imposing centre block of Glasgow's classically turreted Royal Infirmary, opened in 1914; on its original foundation stone is the inscription: 'Erected for healing of diseases of the poor, with money voluntarily contributed by the inhabitants of this city, and other benevolent people in Scotland.' The other is Tennents' Wellpark Brewery. It's not just that the latter—all chimneys and malevolently glinting metal—reminds you of the belching, mill-fevered violence of the city's industrial past (the area in which Necropolis now stands was formerly known as Fir Park—then the air killed the trees after which it was named). There's something else.

On a wall of the brewery, in the shadow of the hill, is a series of brilliantly colourful murals that places pints of lager, and the trademark 'T' of Tennents into unlikely settings.

Across the road, is a pub, The Ladywell, which we passed on our way to Necropolis. The Ladywell is an unlovely-looking boozer, squat, flat-roofed, done out in funereal black. There's a mural on this building too, overlooking the tiny yard and benches that make up its beer garden. This one is of the statue of the Duke of Wellington that stands outside the Museum of Modern Art in the centre of town, complete with iconic traffic cone on its head. The Duke is suggesting it's 'Time for a pint!' but this is no innocent invitation. Whether intentionally or not, his eyes are dark like empty sockets: you are looking at a corpse.

Cader Idris, Gwynedd, Wales

I am supposed to be heading up Cader Idris without a map and have been
dropped off at a layby on the A487 which means I am lost until I come across
four men making camp; they have a bivvy, I think, though I can't be sure. It's
that way, they say, bluff and hale, and point to a sheer face with clumps of
bracken and gorse to hold onto. I thank them for their help and they grin as
I set off. By the time I can't safely go up any further or get back down, I look
over my tensed shoulder into the valley and see they've raised a flag outside
their tent; it is the insignia of the RAF, for whom death, I imagine, is almost
always at a psychic distance, the joshing bastards.

Loch Morar, the Highlands, Scotland

In a space between lockdowns we went on holiday to the north-west coast of Scotland. We were looking for some respite from the overcrowded parks, bad news and frenzied dislocation of COVID, and had heard good things. The drive was long and twisting but it didn't disappoint; with every dark loch and crag from Fort William, and what felt like the last of civilisation, our disposition improved until, cresting the final cloud-swathed incline before the Atlantic, the mist cleared and we were enveloped in a translucent coastal light.

It got better. Our holiday home overlooked an inlet of white beaches enclosed by low hills. The water was still, shimmering. The only human intrusions into the idyll were a tiny jetty and a handful of cottages. After unpacking, we walked down to the beach, in-and-out of coves, towards the ocean. There was a sea eagle. Horsetails and thistle and fern. Three jackdaws flew overhead, and one of the children pointed excitedly at what might have been a seal; the only people we saw were wild campers, a family kayaking in the sunshine, another becalmed on bodyboards, a long way across the hazy stillness of the water. Later, with the sky a full moon-bright, a family of long tailed mice came up to the open glass doors of our patio.

That first night, as we sat and looked out across the inlet, we spoke about what we'd seen. The landscape was glorious, the restorative qualities of unsullied land and sea and air unmatched. And then our considerations turned, as they do these days, to privilege. We knew that here was a place an almost unfathomable distance from the quotidian experience. We also knew that anyone who had the time to research its unspoiled exclusivity—and the money to pay for it—was lucky. Extraordinarily so.

From there our reflections rippled further out into the world, as they do these days, and we drifted into more troubling territory. Was there a correlation, somehow, between the privilege we were enjoying and the condition of the environment? Between the pristine nature of the place and the numbers and demographic of its visitors? Was it unspoiled *because* of its exclusivity? And, if so, what were the implications of this relationship for the conservation of such spaces? And for more, much more besides?

Any discomfort was passing. How could it not be? We slept a sea-air sleep and the next day, the view from the house was breathtaking. The sun glittered off the surface of the inlet and the seaweed around the jetty was an impossible green. When the tide finished sliding out to sea we retraced our steps along the beach, growing more elated with each step.

And then, at the far end of the inlet, before the beach curled round the headland to the ocean, someone saw it. On a tussock, almost like a plinth: a discarded can of coke. Not washed-up, but left there. Thrown away. In itself pristine, its metal bright and proud. A symbol, a cliché, maybe a corrective; either way, a threat.

Montgomery, Powys, Wales

We went away to Montgomery for a weekend and despite—or perhaps because of—the number of Espresso Martinis we drank, struggled to reconcile our idea of the Countryside—wildflower meadows, blue remembered hills, the odd castle—with our day-to-day experience of the countryside—a village shop selling tubs of black garlic, a sewage treatment works, a castle.

Then we realised it didn't matter. A barn owl landed on the fence outside our kitchen window, its face lit by the moon, and it sat there, barely 10 feet away, for fully five minutes, as we stared at it in excited awe and talked about keeping still and keeping quiet and turning off the light, and all of the things we could do—but didn't—to make the environment less distracting and prolong its presence...

Alnwick, Northumberland, England

In Alnwick, there's a second-hand bookshop—Barter Books—which is one of the largest in Europe. It's housed in the old train station and pays homage to this heritage with a model railway running above the shelves; there are also armchairs and open fires. The shop is ramshackle and as tangled in its layout as the paths of your mind when you start to browse. It's impossible to avoid the trappings of a tourist attraction—a café, a sizeable gift shop—but it's also impossible not to be pulled beneath the surface and into the currents and distortions of the printed word.

Barter Books briefly imposed itself on the public consciousness in 2008, when one of a very few test printings of a poster was discovered in a consignment of books bought at auction. The poster said *Keep Calm and Carry On*, and the shop reprinted it in significant numbers. The line was coined to stimulate a sense of uncomplaining resilience in a population enduring the challenges and privations of the Second World War. Its re-emergence however, coinciding as it did with a financial crash and the subsequent ideological violence of austerity, was ill-timed. Trickling down, from the ruling class to the powerless, through the contemporary mythology of the Blitz Spirit and the idea that 'we're all in this together', it has come to represent a very particular kind of subservience, perhaps closer to *Keep Quiet and Suck It Up*.

Alnwick's other principal tourist attraction is the castle and gardens. These are owned by the hereditary peer Ralph Percy, Duke of Northumberland. The castle is open to the public from Spring to Autumn and its primary function as a family residence is evident as you walk, with eyebrows raised, under its high-ceilinged splendour: in a wooden library of a thousand costume dramas, there are bean bags on the floor in front of a large flat screen telly.

Along with their capacity to inspire awe, the gardens have similarly idiosyncratic touches. There is a central multi-layered sweep of fountain and steps —the Grand Cascade—a Poison Garden of toxic plants and a bamboo maze. There's a rose garden and a Barbara Hepworth, on long-term loan from Arts Council England, which somehow seems the wrong way round. And then, tucked away in a corner of the grounds, is a space hymning self-sufficiency and showcasing the best in home-grown fruit and veg: vibrantly coloured onions and cabbages, potatoes and chard, carrots, leeks, apples and berries.

This area is called the Community Garden. In amongst the sheds and cloches and greenhouses are large fibreglass animals. There's a hippo, an anaconda, a tiger, a lion. This would be the most surprising element of the space— what are they doing in an English country garden?—were it not for the staggering hypocrisy of its existence in the first place. Because in 2015 Northumberland Estates, which manages 100,000 acres of land on behalf of the Duke of Northumberland (who just 4 years earlier was worth £315,000,000) revoked the lease on the 3 acre Park Road Allotments in Isleworth, West London. They wanted to build on the land. Since then they have repeatedly appealed against Hounslow Council's rejection of their plans, and it's becoming increasingly difficult to process such knowledge and remain uncompromised by rage.

Digbeth, Birmingham, England

I work on a HelpDesk at Birmingham City University, where I am paid to be friendly. The university is next to Millennium Point, the 'largest landmark millennium project in England outside the capital'. Millennium Point 'enables its visitors and clients to explore ideas, science, education, and technology' and is an integral part of the city's Knowledge Quarter. Birmingham City University used to be Birmingham Poly. I have never fully understood the sense of pride people derive from their place of birth; although I am proud of BCU's School of Art, School of Jewellery, School of Acting, School of Architecture and Birmingham Conservatoire, it has recently expanded its operations by opening a campus in the United Arab Emirates.

The other day, I left work and was walking past Millennium Point when I was accosted by three men. They wore torn clothes and their shoes had holes in and they looked as though they had just shuffled through the Californian dustbowl. They stood in front of me and although they seemed shifty, they were too hollowed-out to cause me any physical concern.

One of the men muttered something but I'm half-deaf and didn't catch it. 'Say again?' I said and he muttered something else and pointed over my shoulder. 'What was that, mate? Dog kennels? You want a dog kennel?' He gave me a look that I didn't want to engage with. 'No, not dogs!' he said, 'food bank! Is there a food bank up here?'

*

The trains that used to go to London from Birmingham left the city over a half a mile of exquisitely engineered Victorian viaduct. You can see the viaduct from BCU, from Millennium Point. Its arches are serene in their permanence, and they seem symbolic somehow, of myths that have long since lost their pull: pride in your work, a sense of community, collegiate and even transnational endeavour. Beneath the arches is Digbeth. Digbeth was once a tightly-packed square mile of redbrick factories and the thriving, bustling pubs and cafes and betting shops of working people. There were Screw Works and Pressed Steel Works, a tea factory, a factory making custard powder, a library and schools. By the side of busy canals sat warehouses. Now most these warehouses are empty; the odd metal spinner or galvaniser excepted, the factories are falling down, windowless and graffitied. Now the district's activity centres on craft ale bars, the odd art gallery and studio, studs of Knowledge Quarter/Creative Content Hub/Enterprise Zone/Big City Plan investment in a rubble-strewn wasteland.

Under a viaduct arch, five minutes from BCU and Millennium Point, is a half-roofed two-storey Victorian factory—PREMIER PLATING TIGS "THE FINISH STARTS HERE"; W.R. PAR   INNER SHEET METAL WORKER ESTD 1921—that sleeps a bevy of the homeless. A couple of years ago I went to a discussion about pan-Europeanism in the Walker Building, a re-purposed warehouse round the corner. Down the road there is a pub called Nortons which boasts 'Not Another Irish Bar.' This is an absurd thing to have on a sign in Digbeth—*in Digbeth!*—whether you are being ironic, or playful, or not.

*

The Birmingham bit of HS2 is being built in front of BCU and Millennium Point, alongside the Victorian arches. The backstreets that are home to the galleries and empty units and derelict buildings of Digbeth are being torn up, wire mesh fencing erected, taken down, erected again. There is lots of signage proclaiming the glory of the development and the benefits it will bring; none that mention it will likely end at Crewe. They are also digging-up Digbeth High Street, building tramlines. I'm not sure where the trams will go to but although it will be nowhere like Digbeth—because there is nowhere like Digbeth—it will also be somewhere exactly the same.

One day, cycling to work along my ever-changing commute, I came to a fence across the road, a diversion along a very short stretch of pavement and a sign saying 'Cyclists Dismount!' There is never anyone around at that time in the morning so I ignored it, and mounted the pavement for 3 seconds or so. Someone in a hi-vis jacket shouted something at me from behind a fence, but I'm half-deaf and didn't catch it. The next day, at the same spot, half a dozen hi-vises blocked my path. There was no-one else around and the stretch of pavement was empty. 'Do you see that sign?' said a big fella, in my face, 'I want you to get off your bicycle.'

At work, I printed and laminated a sign of my own. It said 'BULLYING JOBSWORTH CUNT!' in big letters, and on my way home I hung it on the section of fencing next to 'Cyclists Dismount!' For the next two months I took a longer route to work, and reflected on what people would think of HS2 and the tramlines in 150 years' time. It seems there is an historical/ahistorical inevitability to the dereliction of all things that Digbeth's performative hubris won't help. But then maybe that's just me.

Midsummer Boulevard, Milton Keynes, England

I don't know Milton Keynes well enough to form an opinion on whether it's a triumph of utopian design or the most oppressive end product that utilitarianism has to offer; what I do know is that when you first encounter Midsummer Boulevard—all concrete, and airy, naturally-lit underpasses, wide avenues, and uniform-ish blocks of steel and glass—you know it was put together at a time when how we live and work together was the subject of a serious humanist discourse, not decided by the whims and diktats of a venal plutocracy.

Which makes it all the more dispiriting, of course, that the last thing I saw before veering left to the proud public library, just after the junction with V7 Saxon Street, was someone living in a tent.

Sparkhill, Birmingham, England

I've never been a football fan. I've been lifted off my feet by the crowd at Elland Road and have seen the Baggies and the Blues at home, but I've always disliked the influence that football has over the playground, the pub, the office and the factory floor. I also think there's too much money involved— relative to anything really—and that the connections sport makes between people resemble more closely tribalism than togetherness. I do play though, twice a week.

It's a pick-up game, on the outdoor 7-a-side pitches at Moseley School in Sparkhill. Sometimes there's 4-aside, sometimes 10. The games have been going for about thirty years. We're a mix of ages. At present, a sixty-plus ex-fireman plays regularly, and we have FE tutors, someone who works for the BBC, someone who makes stained glass in the Jewellery Quarter, a full-time carer, part-time furniture up-scaler; comparatively recently, we had a 15 year-old who used to disappear under a scrum of hard-bitten cloggers before emerging with the ball because he trained with West Brom.

We attract passers-by too, locals who come down to the pitches on the off-chance of getting a game. I'm not sure how they got involved but we have a French-speaking Moroccan contingent—all with quick feet and plenty of gas —who are now part of the team; before their arrival, we said goodbye to Habte who moved to another part of the city, and had to bail. Habte was a theology student in his 30's who'd spent a bit of time in Italy before coming to the UK. After he'd been playing for a year or two, he suggested a game with some of his mates, 11-a-side, on a full-sized pitch. One of our lot billed it as a match with 'the Somalian Community' rather than a kick-about with friends, and although we took the piss there's nothing wrong with that, and it might even be the point. Then there's Darius, originally from Iran, back after kids and a knee injury, and Maj who used to play on the pitch next door with the taxi drivers who swear and fight each week, it seems, and Milton, who we told to leave because he moaned too much. Recently we asked a couple of teenaged brothers—Usman and Mehran—to bump up the numbers, and they ran rings round us for a month or so: turned out they were with the Wolves Academy.

We get on. Occasionally there are squarings-off and shouting, the odd two-footed challenge—of course!—because we take it seriously, but twice a year we use the surplus kitty money to pay for a meal out. About 10 years ago, one of our number—the son of a copper, and a county chess first board who'd been playing for 20 years—was diagnosed with eye cancer and not given long to live. He'd been very good, fast and sharp, a natural goal scorer. He played on, either side of having an eye and half his liver removed, even when he couldn't run and kept repeating himself. When he died the football team helped to pack out All Saints Church in Kings Heath; as his coffin left the building and was carried past the tents that had been set-up in the square, for jazz bands and food and drink, 'I'm Forever Blowing Bubbles'—the song of his beloved West Ham United—played.

Tywyn, Gwynedd, Wales

Class runs through this part of Gwynedd like the strata of slate that were blasted out of the ground, and now lie strewn across villages and towns made threadbare by imperialist neglect. This doesn't stop the English from coming though, or from adding to the ambient tension. Year-after-year Gwynedd plays host to two distinct types, those from the council estates of Birmingham and the Black Country, and others in love with Billabong. And, of course, to people somewhere in-between, unsure of their membership of either class. People like us.

We come to Abergynolwyn, a village halfway between the coast and Cader Idris, the mountain that commands the valley of Tal-y-Llyn. Abergynolwyn was built on slate of slate. In the mid-19th century an Irish family of Manchester mill owners bought the ailing mines and provided cottages for the workers. In time the village supported four separate places of worship—on a walking trail you can hear testimony that claims the miners didn't drink or swear and spent their Mondays discussing the sermons of the previous day—and we stay in a converted chapel, the second home of friends of friends.

The chapels aside, there's not much of interest in Abergynolwyn now the pub has shut. It's true people stop off here for the narrow-gauge steam railway, for Cader and the Dolgoch Falls, and there's an annual village show with vegetable-growing competitions for the second-homers, but we prefer to head for the coast, through a slew of faded caravan parks, to the towns of Aberdyfi and Tywyn.

Aberdyfi used to be a busy commercial port, but you wouldn't know it. Today, at least on this side of the river mouth, there's a row of pastel-coloured guest-houses and home-made ice cream parlours and boutique clothes stores. The sand is soft, there's crabbing on the pier and a Victorian viewing platform halfway up a cliff, for looking out across the estuary. Aberdyfi might almost be described as genteel; it's certainly aesthetically pleasing. Tywyn is different. Tywyn is bigger, more complicated.

On the High Street, in amongst the takeaways and the convenience stores with net bags of footballs for the beach, there are shops selling incense and lavender soaps and rocking horses that wouldn't look out of place inland, in boho-quirky Machynlleth, the spiritual centre of the West Wales hippie trail. In a narrow corner of town there's a cinema—The Magic Lantern—that's been showing films since 1900; this is opposite the Salt Marsh Kitchen, a locally-sourced high-end bistro. Yet there are also estates where it's rumoured ex-Brummies take smack. And then, of course, the front.

The front of Tywyn is sandblown. The colour from the B&B's and social housing has been leeched by salty wind. There's a crazy golf course which is always busy, and a concrete open air paddling pool that's dry and muddy. Next to a shack that sells fish and sausage and chips, is a standalone amusement arcade called The Buccaneer. I wanted to take a photo of The Buccaneer, to frame or distil my observation like Martin Parr or Helen Levitt or William Gedney, and I wanted some people in it, preferably playing slot machines while eating a sausage from the shack. I imagined it would be a great pic, a portrait of a typically shabby British seaside resort. But although I'd just played crazy golf I felt uneasy, about staying in a second home in an old chapel, about class, so I waited until there were no people in the shot.

Manchester University, Manchester, England

On my way to the bookshop, I got lost and met Dean. It was dusk and drizzling. I'd walked from the station and, having missed my turn, had arrived at some five-a-side pitches and a distinctly un-campus-like vibe. At a bus stop promising services to Moss Side I turned round and headed back the way I'd come, when a small slight fella came scuttling across the road.

'Nearly got hit there,' he muttered.

'Yeah I saw that,' I said.

We walked together for a few yards then he turned off to the right, back onto the campus and I followed, only vaguely aware of my bearings. 'Where do you want to go?' he said and I said 'Blackwells' and he said 'where?' and I said 'it's near a Brew Dog' and he said 'oh I know where that is. I'm going that way. I'm going to try to make some money. I'll take you there.'

We walked together for about five minutes, chatting away. He told me his name was Dean. I wondered if I should tell him that I knew what it was like to be No Fixed Abode, but every time I said something, he changed the subject. He touched on the implications of a cashless society, how few people gave him money these days, how difficult it was to keep a good spot. He said something about being a 'dependent' which I didn't quite catch. As we turned another corner, he said 'could you get me something for showing you where it is?' and I agreed.

He wanted a big bottle of Stella. I was late for the reading and I checked we wouldn't be going too far. 'There's a Tesco just up here,' said Dean. We walked past Blackwells to a Co-op I'd noticed earlier. As we approached, he indicated a woman sitting on the low wall outside. She looked in a bad way. 'Be careful,' he said 'don't let her see you. She's violent. She'll have it off me' and then, as we left, 'did you see her? Her eyes are all over the place.'

The bookshop was shut. I stood outside, trying to catch the attention of the people inside by force of will, while Dean banged repeatedly on the door. This made me uneasy. I hadn't been to Manchester for 10 years, and had wondered about the wisdom of coming so far for an event. Would people remember me? How—if at all—would I be received? Either way, I wanted to make a good impression. Eventually we were spotted and I was let in. 'Thanks a lot,' said Dean, and he walked off in the direction of the Co-op.

I sat at the back of the room. The readings had already started. Two of the collections—David Frankel's *Forgetting is How We Survive* and David Gaffney's *Concrete Fields*—were about the contrast between living in the city and living in the countryside, and the effects of these environments on their inhabitants' behaviours. One was dark, edgy, the other occasionally surreal. The third book—Clare Fisher's *The Moon is Trending*—touched on another contemporary literary preoccupation, the role played by external perceptions in the construction of your identity.

The host was cheery, the mood jocular. There was a good crowd who asked enthusiastic questions, before power-milling. To my relief, I was greeted with pleasant surprise by the writers and editors of my acquaintance. After the audience Q&A, we went to a bar next door, drank craft lager, snacked and gossiped about publications and rejections and forthcoming projects. I enjoyed basking in this validation, and left myself short of time to get back to the station. When I left, I had to go past the Co-op. By now it was dark. Dean was there, sitting cross-legged on the wall, nursing his bottle. 'Thanks mate' he said as I approached, and I said 'any time.' Then he held out his hand for what I thought was a handshake, but turned out to be a fist bump. I was walking so fast I didn't have time to adjust and ended up grasping his thin wrist firmly, which felt wrong and wasn't, I hoped, interpreted as some sort of power play.

Elie to St Monan's and Pittenweem, Fife, Scotland

Was it the systems of late-Capitalism that had made me sick, or the people that thrived in them? The cumulative effects of decades of low-paid, menial jobs, or my gaffers? Whatever it was, I don't think I'd ever been in more need of a break.

I'd been off work for 4 weeks with stress, a condition that had become apparent when I'd sent another non-collegiate email to one of my many line managers. I'd been working on a Helpdesk at a small university, earning just above minimum wage, forced to endure both the crushingly repetitive tasks that made up my daily routine, and prolonged exposure to the weakeners I worked with, colleagues at higher pay grades who only seemed to come alive when reminding me of my inconsequentiality. There had been questions for me to consider—did my responses show that I was too quick to anger? Was I ground down, or merely a misanthrope?—but what was inescapable were the effects of day-after-day of incremental degradation, my intolerance of people who surrendered to petty hierarchies, and the need to do something about it.

We arrived at Elie late in the afternoon, after a long drive from Alnwick in Northumberland. The only break in the journey had come at a Starbucks in Dreghorn. We were staying on the narrow seafront. There was a cafe overlooking the bay, a pub—The Ship Inn—and an art gallery. The tide was out, the beach flat and early dusk-lit. The scene was simplicity itself, serenely bustling simplicity. So taken was I by the sight that greeted us, it took a while to register that the place was full of second-homers, I mean I'd rarely seen so many nautically-striped shirts and tasselled deck shoes and four-by-fours in such a confined space.

No matter. The next morning, I woke to a cloudless sky, to herring gulls and the sea. I breathed deep. My plan—a plan I'd been nurturing for weeks now —was to find the coastal path that passed through Elie, and walk. Just walk. I didn't know where it would take me but I didn't care; all that concerned me was escaping the psychic violence of the familiar and the full of shit.

From a motor home park-up overlooking another tiny bay, I set off through thick bracken. The path went past a lighthouse, before it reached the shore and opened-up, threading between pastureland, and rocky beaches of thick sand and seaweed.

> *Here's someone coming the other way. Path's a bit narrow...I'll just wait here.*

> *Good morning!*

> *Good morning!*

It was waymarked with signage decorated with puffins and shellfish. Walkers were advised to look out for the Brown Angus butterfly and report any they saw. I peered into the clear light towards the sea: sitting on the shimmering rocks at the very edge of the land, was what looked like a cormorant, and I could feel my face was creased with the exhilaration of it all.

> *Someone else—look like locals—catch their eye and—hello!*

> *Hello!*

About half a mile from Elie I went past a sign for a farm shop, and made a note to return at some point, buy some local honey. But not today. Today I was walking. By now the path had started to rise and fall more expressively. The beaches had been replaced by jagged linear strata of volcanic rock, and the simple restorative effects of the landscape—the grasses and breeze, the seabirds, the space—were embroidered by something more, the contemplative appeal of the human unfamiliar. I passed a derelict, unnamed building, and then, rising over a thicket of thrift and daisies and thistle that was grow-ing at the bottom of a flight of wooden steps, I saw another, the ruin of a castle.

They're not local, not dressed like that. Where can I go? Not quite enough room there... haven't I just passed somewhere—ah yes that'll do...whoah careful!—and smi... oh. Ignore me then. Bit rude.

Round the next rise-and-fall of the path, I saw the witch's hat of a spire, emerg-ing from a cornfield. It disappeared from view and then I was at the building it belonged to, a robust old church: another sign told me this was the 14th century St Monan's kirk, the place of worship closest to the sea in all of Scotland.

Morning!

Good morning!

Beautiful day!

It is, it is! You see? That's the way to do it? Not hard is it?

The path continued, skirting the seaweed-covered foundations of the church before taking me past a couple of cottages and up a narrow flight of steps lined with rosebay and teasels. From there it wound steeply through the town itself, disappearing and reappearing between rows of pastel-coloured terraces and alleyways before dropping down to the working harbour. The tide was out and the boats in the quay sat in mud. One becalmed boat was bright orange and called Defiance.

Obviously posh. A train of posh. Might be nice posh? No, still no eye contact, not from any of them, even though I perched myself on that rock so they could sweep past, like they had some divine right-of-way.

Coming out of St Monan's were the remains of a saltworks. There wasn't much left beyond grassy mounds of earth but the windmill that had been used to grind the mineral had been restored and there fellow walkers gath-ered; there were more people still in the tidal pool at the edge of town—a briny-cold dip, deep-set in the dark volcanic rock—and then I was back on the coastal path proper.

More posh. Crew Clothing, polo shirts. Yep. Thought as much. You're welcome.

From St Monan's the landscape changed. On the landward-side of the path were steep banks, dense with vegetation; out to sea, the rocks were no longer black but a rusty deep red. Although there had been butterflies all along the route, now it seemed as though I was walking through clouds of them. I wondered if this had something to do with a change in flora, but I didn't know enough about the species that surrounded me to be sure. I felt the same—a wonder-filled curiosity—when I saw a pale yellow bird staring at me from a thicket; it wasn't until I saw an illustration on the next sign that I realised it had been a yellowhammer. A yellowhammer!

A waymarker said it was ½ a mile to a town called Pittenweem. That would mean I'd walked about 4 miles. On the outskirts of the town was another tidal pool, with seals stretched on the rocks alongside. I climbed to a viewing point where people were looking out for bottlenose whales. It was next to a desultory crazy golf course, which seemed apposite, somehow. Standing there, I suddenly felt the jolts and undulations of the walk in my legs and decided to head back to Eli. There was time for Pittenweem another day. I'd certainly be back along the path; I'd enjoyed my introduction to Fife, but part of me suspected it still had work to do.

Wankers! Cough-wankers-cough. Too loud? Fuck it, see if I care, you snotty, entitled fuckers!

Come on Ollie!

Yeah, come on Ollie, you little prick!

Leicester, England

That morning, travelling from Birmingham to De Montfort University, I was thinking about how to write, as I often did.

I had for some time believed the key to effective writing was to concentrate on the surface of things. Record them faithfully, and they'd do the work for you. After all, the world is manifestly absurd and provides you with everything you need in the way of character and environment and plot; why complicate—or simplify—things with undue authorial mediation?

Recently however, I had started to question the value of such an approach. Living through the shitstorm—the onset of a Sixth Extinction, a possible civilisation-ending war, a global pandemic—in a society where inequality threatens to become an existential crisis, and the language of what passes for our public discourse causes potentially irreparable damage to the institutions on which our functioning depends, I began to wonder if I should do more than this. If I should, perhaps, be more explicitly critical, more obviously critically engaged. Maybe circumstances like ours need more than the baldly representational to draw out the unique truths of their car-crash lunacy. Maybe it was time for me to choose sides, respond in kind to the nature of the challenges we face, and shift from mere observer to judge, from viewer to participant.

It was a tricky question and I was none the wiser by South Wigston. As I arrived at Leicester, I had abandoned the prospect of a resolution and my contemplations were back on more prosaically quotidian territory. I was working as a Fellow with the Royal Literary Fund, advising students on their academic writing, and my day was due to include talking to a postgrad doing a Dissertation in Advanced Biomedical Science, and undergrads with assignments in Nursing and Environmental Law. Typically demanding, typically satisfying, it came and went. The clocks had just gone back and by the time I left campus, evening was seeping into the city, I was tired, and wanted to get home.

Back at Leicester station I made the train with time to spare. I'd been sitting in my seat for 10 minutes when the first announcement was made. We were unable to leave the station because of an 'incident' at Birmingham New Street. There was a carriage-wide fumble for news which revealed the cause of delay was a 'suspect device'. New Street and the surrounding area had been evacuated; on Twitter, people were running. It didn't look promising and sure enough, 10 minutes later, we were advised to keep hold of our tickets and use them to travel the following day.

I looked out at the platform. It was murky and had just started to rain. I had appointments the next day, no change of clothes or toiletries, and my response to the news was annoyance. By the time I'd walked out of the station however, my frustration had given way to anticipation. After all, I did have a half-empty notebook in my bag, and it had been a long time since I'd spent an impromptu night in an unfamiliar city, longer still since I'd had the time and headspace to anything more than just think about my own writing.

I Googled a Premier Inn, made my way there through the drizzle. The Premier Inn had no spaces and I was told to try the Ibis. The route took me along a short stretch of one of the A roads that encircle the city centre. The Ibis was at a busy intersection. It stood in isolation at the top of an incline, on what looked like a traffic island, five Ballardian stories rising half-lit from the gloom. I booked a room.

The rain was heavier as I set off in search of what I needed for the next day. I found my way to Granby Street, where the lights from shop windows twinkled unconvincingly. By now I was wet through and bedraggled. Sweaty too, sweatier than I should have been in November. In Boots, as I looked for a toothbrush, I was followed by a shop assistant; the same thing happened in M&S as I browsed their underwear. I imagined I would be reimbursed for the price of my room but mindful of how much Ibis were charging for a generic Euro-bland bar meal, I bought a tub of up-to-its date taramasalata, a bread roll and a banana for my tea; in Barnardo's I plumped for a four quid denim shirt rather than a more formal number for twice the price.

On my way back to the Ibis, I passed groups of youths loudly blocking the pavement outside fried chicken joints. There were pound shops next to South Indian restaurants, wet sleeping bags in doorways, some full of beggar. At a sawdust-floored pub called The Barley Mow, I stopped for a pint. There was a pool table. I thought about putting a coin down, playing a few racks, introducing myself to new friends and drinking partners, but the Guinness didn't hit the spot and my university shoes and cords combo had attracted the attention of two blokes in hi-viz jackets, so I left.

I arrived back at my room, ate my food. The taramasalata had a tang. As I lay on the bed, I took out my notepad, chewed on my pen and thought about how I'd spent the last hour-and-a-half. I was determined to make the most of the opportunity and write about the experience, but how?

At first, I thought I'd been presented with an answer to the question I'd been considering that morning. I thought I could see what I had to do. The evening had introduced me to the implacability, the relentlessness of things. After all, there were homeless people in Birmingham too. There were middle-class supermarkets, and charity shops, and sceptical punters in rough pubs, the weather was too hot for the time of year and it rained. I could be intimidated, buy old fish dip. All that viewing these experiences in a different environment had done was show me that the mere observance and, by logical if creative extension, the mere recording of life was subject to the law of diminishing returns. And that if my writing was to respond effectively to the world, I did indeed need to do more, to dig beneath the surface of things, to immerse myself in the challenge. But the day had one last development, one final exquisitely superficial detail to compound my to-ings-and-fro-ings.

Putting down my pen for a moment, I returned to my phone. New Street station was open again after hours of disruption. And the suspect device that had brought chaos to the centre of the UK's second city? A cannabis grinder that had been mistaken for a grenade.

The author

Charlie Hill is a writer from Birmingham, who left school at 16 to work in the Bull Ring fish market. He then spent decades in-and-out of minimum-waged work and years with no fixed abode or precariously housed.

He started writing on buses and in the pub and his first novel was published in 2010. He now works as a Fellow for the Royal Literary Fund. He likes to take risks with his prose; fans include the novelist and short story writer Carys Bray, who has said 'Hill renders the ordinary extraordinary', and the poet and novelist Neil Campbell: 'Charlie Hill is a poet of suburbia.'

Charlie still lives in Birmingham, though he is happiest up a fell or near the sea.

BV - #0058 - 170724 - C20 - 210/148/3 - PB - 9781912710744 - Matt Lamination